Safeguarding Children

from

Domestic Abuse

An Introductory Guide
for Professionals

Kate Hennessey Bowers

This book is presented in the dyslexia-friendly font Century Gothic.

Contents

Dedication

To my community, my sisters and brothers - survivors. You are braver than you know, worth more than you can imagine and loveable beyond belief... But believe it!

We are here for each other.

INTRODUCTION

How does a seventeen year old, A* student, find herself leaving home to live in a violent, abusive, exploitative relationship with a man twice her age?

An interesting question...

With many complex answers. But let me share with you just a small part of this experience.

I wasn't diagnosed with ADHD until I was thirty three.
I didn't learn about rejection sensitive dysphoria until two years after that.
I didn't realise that I am Autistic until I was thirty seven.
I didn't know about attachment styles until I became a mother.
I didn't know about child criminal exploitation until I became a teacher.
I didn't know about Adverse Childhood Experiences until I became a Safeguarding Officer.

I didn't know about domestic abuse until I was seventeen when this became my own, lived, experience. When all of the things that I mentioned above became my reality. Physical and sexual violence, coercion and control, exploitation and emotional abuse were my life for three years. I am still not sure that a person can really *know* domestic abuse until they have *lived* it, but we *can* all try to understand it, we *can* all try to raise awareness of it and we *can* all try to prevent it.

I had been an A* student, Head Girl of my high school, captain of the Netball team and keen to learn, do and impress. Nevertheless, I was socially awkward, extremely naïve and desperate to feel loved. By the time I had started college, I was confused about myself, like most teenagers. I was dabbling with risky behaviour, pushing the boundaries and seeking a sense of belonging.

He was attractive, charming, clever and an experienced abuser of teenage girls and women.

It wasn't like there weren't warning signs. There were plenty, some discreet; like the way he behaved in private, the underhand comments to make me question myself and his lack of stability in his circumstances which he blamed on his ex-girlfriend. None of which I could see at the time. Then there were also very clear signs, ex-boyfriends calling me to warn me about him, which I was encouraged to believe was because they were jealous. His ex-girlfriends called to tell me about him, which again he convinced me were lies because of their jealousy.

When you feel desperate to be loved, to be seen and to be a part of something, your subconscious has the power to tell you that this unsettled feeling that you have means nothing. Or worse - you buy into the misconception that butterflies are a sign of infatuation! When neurodivergent children spend years masking and shutting down their natural instincts in order to "fit in", they learn to distrust themselves. In my case, both proved to be detrimental to the next three years of my life.

I *could* tell you the whole story here; the first time he hit me, the first time he kicked me, the time he beat me in front of his brothers and their children, the times that he hit me in public, the rape, the drugs, the painful and damaging interactions with the police, the last time he strangled me. But there isn't enough space in this introduction for the whole *story*. That's for another book entirely. (Maybe?) However, I will include some of my experiences throughout the book, where relevant.

What I do want you to know is that my experience as a child victim of domestic abuse means that I am a survivor. I am an advocate for other victims and survivors of domestic abuse. I am a voice for children who experience domestic abuse. And you can be too. You don't need to be a survivor to be able to see, hear and respond to the experiences of children.

When we work restoratively with other agencies, with communities, with families and with children directly, we create safe spaces for vulnerability to be shared. And in doing so we create safe spaces for people to thrive and for positive lasting change.

At any given moment you have the power to say this is not how the story is going to end.
- Christine Mason Miller

CHAPTER ONE
What is Domestic Abuse?

Domestic abuse is defined as any type of narcissistic, coercive, controlling or threatening behaviour, violence, stalking or abuse between people who are either currently in a relationship (not always romantic or sexual) or have previously been, regardless of their gender or sexuality. It can include emotional, psychological, sexual, physical or financial abuse.

The definitions of domestic abuse vary across the globe, therefore it is essential for professionals to obtain clarity from their national and local guidance as to the most current definition that they must adopt in their role of preventing domestic abuse and safeguarding children.

So let's define some of those terms, what exactly does it mean to be coercive? What might a threat look like? In the following captions, we will explore this.

Coercion and control

According to the UK Government coercive behaviour is an act or a pattern of acts of assault, threats, humiliation and intimidation or other abuse that is used to harm, punish, or frighten their victim.

Controlling behaviour is defined as a range of acts designed to make a person subordinate and/or dependent by isolating them from sources of support, exploiting their resources and capacities for personal gain, depriving them of the means needed for independence, resistance and escape and regulating their everyday behaviour.

"If you go out with your friends tonight, I am going to tell everyone that you are a lazy bitch and a shit mum"

"Give me that money or I'll hurt you!"

As a survivor of domestic abuse, I (along with many others) would also refer to the less overt examples of coercion. The covert, the type that can often look (to the unhealed or untrained eye) kindness...

"If you stay at home with me, instead of seeing your friends I will buy you new clothes"

"I'll love you more when you start doing what I say!"

"You can have your keys back when you've cleaned that up"

Threatening behaviour

Collins dictionary refers to threatening behaviour as "intimidation or intentional behaviour that causes another person to fear injury or harm". Similar to and potentially present in coercion and control but more specifically, in terms of the law, referring to the threat of physical harm.

"I'm going fucking kill you when we get in!"
"You deserve a good kicking."

Narcissistic behaviour

Refers to the abuse perpetrated by a person with a narcissistic personality (diagnosed as a disorder or not). Some common examples of narcissistic abuse include:

- Withholding: This can be money, affection, or even communication in an attempt to punish their victim.
- Insults: Verbal abuse such as insults, harsh criticism, etc. serve to diminish the victims self esteem, even when disguised as jokes.
- Emotional blackmail: Using guilt, shame or fear to get the victim to comply.
- Malicious gossip: Spreading lies about the victim to intentionally harm their reputation to isolate them.
- Sabotage: Damaging a victim's relationship with work, friends or other aspects of their life to maintain power.
- Accusations: Deflecting negative attention from themselves by accusing their victim of any kind of negative behaviour.

Domestic abuse can include emotional, psychological, sexual, physical or financial abuse:

Emotional
- taking control over elements of someone's everyday life, such as what they wear and where they go
- trapping a person, not letting them leave the house

Psychological
- threatening to kill or harm them or harm a partner, friend, family member or pet.
- removing privacy by reading emails, text messages or letters
- gaslighting, intentionally leading a person to self-doubt and confusion
- stalking; harassment or obsessive unwanted attention

Sexual
- sexual behaviour or a sexual act forced upon a person without their consent

- sexual harassment and rape (including within a relationship)

Physical

- punching, kicking, cutting, hitting with an object, poisoning, drugging, strangling

Financial

- withholding money or preventing a person from earning or receiving money
- diminishing a person's financial capacity, in order to create dependency

Domestic abuse can happen at any time, to anyone. Regardless of social class, occupation, education, gender, race, religion, age (although the law now refers to anyone ages sixteen or older).

I think this, this truth, is very hard for people to believe and this is one of many barriers to victims of domestic abuse reporting their abuser or even ending the abuse (I intentionally used the word "ending" as opposed to "leaving" because for the majority of parents - the abuse continues long after they have left the cohabitation arrangement). Unfortunately, this is also a very common tool for manipulation on the part of the perpetrator, after all "who would believe that... fill in the utterly discrediting blank which opposes mainstream stereotypes here!

Nonetheless, there are periods in the annual calendar that statistically evidence an increased number of domestic abuse incidents and therefore greater risk. Typically, the data demonstrates that reports of domestic abuse increase during major football tournaments and Christmas. There are multiple factors that influence this including elevated stress levels, alcohol consumption and increased contact time.

Witnessing and/or experiencing domestic abuse

Domestic abuse has a significant and detrimental impact on children. Witnessing or experiencing it is traumatic and what we often refer to as an "Adverse Childhood Experience" which we now understand will have a damaging effect on children as they age for many years to come or, if left untreated, forever. The exposure to the domestic abuse of a parent, sibling or any other person is categorised as child abuse.

Experiencing domestic abuse as a child can be direct, by seeing and witnessing the abuse, first hand. However, it can also be experienced indirectly. This may look like:

- hearing abuse take place from another room or even from outside or via a device such as a mobile phone or tablet
- being injured from trying to defend the victim or end the abuse
- seeing someone that they love being hurt, belittled, injured and/or distressed
- coming across damage to their environment such as broken furniture, smashed items, defaced belongings
- not having their needs met by their parents or carers, also known as neglect, due to the impairment of capacity due to the abuse (Holt, Buckley and Whelan, 2008). These can be physical, emotional, or educational needs, for example

Children have said that...

"Things would be smashed, there'd be holes in the wall and my dad was quite unpredictable in what he would do and, yeah, it just wasn't right. And we were, the plan ideally would have been for him to move out, because there's obviously more of us than him but he refused that so my mum had to take it into her own hands and that's why we moved." – 16 year old boy

"I mean I couldn't understand it – like I kinda thought maybe this is something that some other people go through as well – like this is just a normal thing – like people drink, stuff like this happens so I kinda took it upon myself that stuff happens that I can't do anything about I'm only 11/12 – however old I was – there's nothing I can really do." – 16 year old girl

"He [Dad] shouts at mummy a lot as well. It made me feel sad. I couldn't do anything because they were just shouting over me and [sisters]. When we was trying to say we're upset, they said, they just kept, carried on shouting." – 8 year old girl

"It's a tense environment as the police is coming and then even though my dad does all these things I'm still really, I feel quite sorry for him, that he has to go through all this even though it is his fault but I just feel so guilty afterwards." – 10 year old girl

"I had to take over from mum if she was tired or something happened... I used to cook a lot. Not so much for me and mum, usually just for me, but I did make it, mum did make me dinner on occasion, I don't know three or four times a week, but the rest of the times I would make my own." – 12 year old boy

Are we listening to them? Do we have a strong sense of what a day in their life looks like - from their perspective? If not, we need to move mountains to understand and capture their voice. Their experiences. Their lived trauma. Their happy times. Their worries. Their grief and pain. Even when they may be unable (never unwilling) to speak for themselves.

We will come back to the voice of the child throughout this guide, exploring the culture in our settings, barriers, environmental, physical, behavioural and more, tools that we can adopt and the impact of empowering children to use their voices restoratively.

Statistics

Domestic abuse only became illegal in the UK in 1976 when the Domestic Violence and Matrimonial Proceedings Act came into place. In over twenty two countries worldwide, abuse - including hitting a spouse or partner is still legal.

The Office of National Statistics (ONS) reports that, in the UK alone, over 2.4 million aged 16 plus are estimated to have experienced domestic abuse in 2022. That's almost 6% of the 41.6 million people in that age group.

According to the Early Intervention Foundation, around 400,000 children across the UK were impacted by domestic abuse in 2022.

According to ONS, 29% of domestic abuse victims are male and the highest proportion of people experiencing domestic abuse are female between the age of 30 and 34 while the greatest proportion of male victims are older, aged 75 and above.

A UK based charity, called MSI Reproductive Choices, reported that they had "seen a 33% increase in domestic violence reports, as the unprecedented lockdown restrictions force women to isolate with their abusers."

Women's Aid UK shares that between January 2005 and August 2015 (inclusive) 19 children and two women were killed by perpetrators of domestic abuse in circumstances relating to child contact

Coordinated Action Against Domestic Abuse (CAADA) reports that 62% of children exposed to domestic abuse are also "severely" directly harmed.

In safeguarding terms, the presence of mental ill health, substance misuse and domestic violence in a single household is known as the "toxic trio". According to Brandon et al (2012), an analysis of 139 serious case reviews showed that one or more of the "toxic trio" played a significant part in 86% of incidents where children were seriously harmed or died, Almost two thirds of these incidents featured domestic abuse and in 6 out of 10 mental ill health was a factor for one or both parents. One quarter of the children experienced all three elements of the "toxic trio".

During 2022 the ONS recorded the factors involved in children being placed on a Child in Need plan under Section 17 of the Children's Act. They reported that 57,260 children who were harmed as a result of domestic abuse, 160,690 children witnessed a parent be abused by an intimate partner and 27,310 children witnessed another adult as a victim of domestic violence. A total of 245,260 children were safeguarded under a child protection plan. A further 669 children were considered to be at risk of significant harm, at the level of Child Protection.

Today he strangled me.

I said that I didn't want to drive him there again, we argued and he grabbed me by the throat. He slammed the back of my head against the wall over and over.

I think I passed out for a moment.

When I opened my eyes I could see his little girl standing over me crying. She had wet herself. She was terrified. But not for herself -

for me.

I don't want mummy to go out with Daddy. When they come back from going the pub they always argue. Mummy cries and Daddy throws things at Mummy.

Mummy's phone got broken.

Mummy had to go the hospital one time because her nose was bleeding and her head was cut and bleeding everywhere.

I cried.

But mummy came back.

ACTIVITY ONE

Look carefully at your own beliefs and those around you. Take time to answer these with deep, honest reflection before seeking external input. Once you have had time to question yourself and journal, take these questions to a peer, or several and discuss your collective views.

Are there ways in which you believe that punishment, emotional, psychological or physical, is acceptable and/or effective? How do you express these beliefs? Within yourself or with others? Or both?

When it comes to punishment, how do we know where the line is between acceptable and unacceptable? How do we help children to navigate this?

Are there messages in professional practice that support the idea of control, coercion, punishment etc as a means to achieving a desired outcome?

What alternative narratives around control and/or punishment do you provide for the children that you support (all children, not just those who have experienced abuse)?

What does healthy conflict resolution look like to you? How is that demonstrated within your practice?

Chapter One Notes

Chapter One Notes

[She] herself does not know she is being abused, because of all the people who say "If it was that bad, you'd leave".
- Survivor

CHAPTER TWO
UK Legislation around domestic abuse

Key legislation
In England, Northern Ireland and Wales legislation states that "seeing or hearing the ill-treatment of another person" is a form of harm (Section 120. Adoption and Children Act 2002; Section 28. Family Homes and Domestic Violence (Northern Ireland) Order 1998).

In England, the Domestic Abuse Act 2021 defines children as victims of domestic abuse if they "see, hear or otherwise experience the effects of abuse". Within this Act there is a duty placed on local authorities to provide safe accommodation such as refuges to support all victims of domestic abuse.

In Scotland, legislation the definition of child abuse includes domestic abuse (Section 24. Family Law (Scotland) Act 2006). Furthermore, the Domestic Abuse (Scotland) Act 2018 defines domestic abuse which involves or affects a child as a statutory aggravation (including a child seeing, hearing, or being present during an abuse).

Guidance

Statutory guidance emphasises the responsibility of all people in the education, care and community sectors to safeguard children from all forms of abuse and neglect, including domestic abuse. As a person who works with children or parents, or in a setting where children or parents may be present, we all have a duty to be familiar with and act in accordance with the most up to date Child Protection Guidance in our country of residence. To access this information simply type the phrase "child protection England / Wales / Scotland / Northern Ireland" into a search engine or go onto your Local Safeguarding Children Board or Partnership website and find the latest National and Local Legislation and Guidance there.

In 2021, the Home Office published a paper called "Tackling violence against women and girls strategy", with a view to:
- increase support for victims and survivors
- increase the number of perpetrators brought to justice
- increase reports to the police
- reduce the prevalence of violence against women and girls.

In 2022 the Violence Against Women and Girls Strategy made over 50 additional commitments including ones specific to domestic abuse such as:

- Supporting teachers to cover the subject sensitively
- An increase in the number of Independent Domestic Violence Advisers
- Invest in programmes to better understand perpetrators of Domestic Abuse in order to prevent it more

The updated strategy also goes on to suggest that future developments will include:

- publishing the UK's first ever standalone Domestic Abuse Plan which will complement the Tackling VAWG Strategy and drive change in the response to this crime, prevention, victim support and conviction
- publishing statutory guidance on domestic abuse to signpost professionals to resources, help them to understand the impact of domestic abuse on victims and highlight best practice

Alongside the Tackling Violence Against Women and Girls paper, the Home Office in England also released factsheets on the measures included in the Domestic Abuse Act 2021 which you can find using the references at the back of this book. The factsheets include information regarding why the measures are needed and the impact that they are intended to have.

Prior to this, in 2018, the Convention of Scottish Local Authorities (COSLA) and Scottish Government published a strategy called "Equally safe: Scotland's strategy to eradicate violence against women". It aims to prevent and eliminate violence against women and girls in Scotland.

The Department of Justice and the Department of Health, Social Services and Public Safety (DHSSPS) in Northern Ireland have published a strategy for challenging sexual and domestic violence and abuse. The strategy aims to raise awareness of and outcomes for the emotional and psychological needs of children who have experienced domestic violence and abuse. The approach includes an annual action plan.

As aforementioned, it is everybody's responsibility to stay up to date with Legislation and Guidance, in order to ensure that our practice is aligned with both national and local policy, procedure and resources and referral pathways. You can keep up-to-date easily by signing up to CASPAR, the NSPCC's automated awareness service.

For Education professionals it's also worth being aware that there are sometimes sub-documents or specific guidance that applies to Education settings, Again, the NSPCC and most Local Authorities have specific newsletters or network groups that can be signed up to receive updates.

ACTIVITY TWO

Use the following page as a checklist to retrieve, read, reflect upon and store the following documents (where applicable). Then make notes about which of them need to be disseminated within your organisation or team and what sort of strategy you could/do adopt to help all staff and volunteers stay updated frequently and discuss domestic abuse regularly to refresh organisation wide understanding.

Checklist:
- Local Safeguarding Children Board or Partnership Policy
- Domestic Abuse Act (England)) 2021
- Section 24. Family Law (Scotland) Act 2006).
- Domestic Abuse (Scotland) Act 2018

- Adoption and Children Act (Northern Ireland) 2002; Section 28.
- Family Homes and Domestic Violence (Northern Ireland) Order 1998
- Home Office, England, Tackling Violence Against Women and Girls paper, 2022
- Home Office, England, Domestic Abuse Act 2021
- Home Office, England Factsheets on the measures included in the Domestic Abuse Act 2021
- Scottish Local Authorities (COSLA) and Scottish Government published a strategy called "Equally safe: Scotland's strategy to eradicate violence against women".
- The Department of Justice and the Department of Health, Social Services and Public Safety (DHSSPS) in Northern Ireland strategy for challenging sexual and domestic violence and abuse.

Local Domestic Abuse professional contacts/phone numbers

How we regularly update staff around policy/legislation/guidance.

How we could/already facilitate regular discussions to raise awareness of domestic abuse:

Chapter Two Notes

Chapter Two Notes

The effects of abuse are devastating and far-reaching. Domestic violence speaks many languages, has many colours and lives in many different communities
- Sandra Pupatello

CHAPTER THREE
Understanding the Impact of domestic abuse

Any form of abuse comprises a child's basic need for security and safety. Domestic abuse is no different, in fact, it directly affects a child's core safety, their home.

According to Holt, Buckley and Whelan, 2008, Stanley, 2011 and Szilassy et al, 2017, domestic abuse has a detrimental effect on their nervous system and brain development which in turn impacts their behaviour, educational outcomes, growth and overall well being.

Attachment

The term "*attachment*" refers to the relationship bond between a child and their primary caregiver. It is a bond that is formed in the early years and has been evidenced to have a long-term impact on a person's sense of self, their behaviour, development, growth and future relationships with others. Usually, a child's primary place and person for love and safety is their primary home and carer, therefore it is extremely confusing and conflicting to experience domestic abuse. The impact of this internal (often expressed externally) conflict can be:

- having an insecure attachment (bond) with their parents or carers
- despite the need for safety and security, the child is likely to have concerns about parental separation
- nonetheless hoping the abused parent or carer will leave to secure safety
- seeking love, affection, attention from their parents (like all children
- whilst being afraid of their parents or carers.

Psychological impact

There are both short and long term psychological effects of experiencing domestic abuse for both adults and children of all ages, the way that these represent themselves will be different depending on the individual child, their age, stage of development, degree of exposure, gender etc. These effects could include (but not limited to):

- aggression and challenging behaviour - this may look like tantrums in some children or fighting with others, sometimes it may look like persistent pushing of boundaries, despite support being in place.
- Depression - this can vary from being withdrawn to chronic tiredness, to persistent irritability
- anxiety - this often looks like worry, fear, tearfulness, bedwetting, difficulty focussing, avoidance of simple tasks or usual enjoyment
- changes in mood - engagement or emotional regulation
- difficulty interacting with others - in different settings, with adults and/or peers, family and extra-familiar
- fearfulness, including fear of conflict, fear of getting things wrong - perfectionism, resistance to change or visible fear of certain types of people or personality types (in particular authoritarian)
- suicidal thoughts or feelings - all of which need to be listened to and taken very seriously
- self harm - this can involve cutting, poisoning, over/under eating, picking, biting, hitting walls, drug/alcohol misuse, hair pulling, unsafe sex and more

Many children, including teenagers, worry that being brought up in an abusive environment will impact their own future relationships. One young person contacted the NSPCC Childline service and reported:

"I have seen my parents physically hurting each other for years. I used to cry every day and self-harm. I feel like I'm really affected by what I've seen. I have a boyfriend now and I feel like he's acting just like my dad. I feel like I can never be in a stable relationship."

Developmental impact

Traumatic or Adverse Childhood Experiences (Otherwise known as ACEs), including domestic abuse, are known to affect a child's brain development.

If children are exposed to prolonged or repeated traumatic experiences, such as domestic violence, this can cause 'toxic' or 'harmful' stress.

Imagine that every child's brain has something similar to a thermostat inside of it, but instead of helping to maintain an optimal temperature, like your heating thermostat at home, the one inside our brains is trying to maintain a baseline level of stress hormones. When the traumatic events are repeated and/or the level of harm increases, the thermostat baseline is pushed higher and higher. Therefore children start to feel more stressed more frequently and for longer periods. This can disrupt the building of healthy brain structure and development, which in turn affects:

- behaviour
- communication
- executive function (the ability to understand, plan, execute tasks)
- emotional regulation
- physical growth
- digestion
- puberty
- and so much more.

When I was 13 I was, like, really stressed, and having a lot of anxiety. I was self – harming myself, and I was trying to commit suicide and stuff... I was causing myself to throw up so I was diagnosed with bulimia – and that was due to stress and not feeling confident in myself – and not feeling happy with anything that was going on – Yeah I think that was the two major things I have ever done to myself to try and cope. – 16 year old girl

ACTIVITY THREE

Think about your role, your setting, your practice, and the children that you have an impact on. Are there ways in which you could improve the way that you create space for them to be seen, heard and understood?

Reflect on your previous experiences where children or young people have been "difficult" to engage, what did that look like?

On these occasions, what may have been going on for them? What might their behaviour have been an indicator of?

Are there messages in professional practice that you have seen, or expressed yourself, that share an expectation that children simply "put aside" their problems so that they can engage?

Given what you have read here about the brain and how trauma impacts it, what are your thoughts on a child's capacity to conduct themselves as required by a setting as opposed to how their brain/body has been "wired"?

What would you want to change about your own practice to create a space where children who have experienced domestic abuse can thrive and feel safe to build trusting relationships?

Chapter Three Notes

Chapter Three Notes

Domestic abuse happens only in intimate, interdependent, long-term relationships – in other words, in families – the last place we would want or expect to find violence.

– Leslie Morgan Steiner

CHAPTER FOUR

Recognising domestic abuse

Domestic abuse can take place in any relationship, regardless of gender, age (although, as we already discussed, the law refers to it as 16+), race, culture, religion, sexuality etc. It can continue and often does continue, long after the relationship has ended. For many parents, contact with the other parent who is also an abuser, whether via mediation, phone call, social media, or in person, the abuse is prolonged.

When domestic abuse victims leave a relationship, we (often mistakenly) assume they are safe. However, Domestic Shelters (2022) reports that "*90% of coercive control victims report experiencing post-separation abuse (PSA). Post-separation abuse often harms domestic abuse victims for years or decades after separation.*"

All kinds of people can be abusers. We know there is a prevalence in the data towards certain profiles, as seen in chapter two, but when we see potential signs of domestic abuse, we cannot leave room for assumption and prejudice. One way of reducing this is to maintain professional curiosity. This refers to exploring every possible indicator of abuse through open and respectful questions. It is underpinned by the desire to understand what the life of the child is like on a day to day basis – including their routines and relationships and their thoughts and feelings.

Risk and vulnerability factors

The following information captions look carefully at a variety of factors for risk and vulnerability around domestic abuse:

Connections with other forms of abuse

According to Stanley, 2011, *"If a child lives in a home where domestic abuse is happening, they're more at risk of other types of abuse"*.

AACADA states that *"One third [of perpetrators AND victims experiencing domestic abuse] disclose mental health issues and/or substance misuse"*

Their studies also revealed that 62 % of children who experienced domestic abuse had also experienced physical abuse directly themselves.

Signs and indicators

It can be difficult to identify if domestic abuse is taking place because perpetrators often behave very differently when other people are around. This is in part, to uphold a reputation or demeanour of being a *"good"* person so that others like and trust them, but there is another factor.

Another key element of narcissistic and/or controlling/abusive behaviour involves convincing their victim that they, the perpetrator, are worthy of their love and the abuse is *"out of character"* for them. In fact, it further gaslights the victim into believing that they have brought the abuse upon themselves and are to blame. Further diminishing their self esteem and self worth, meaning that they are increasingly more likely to *"accept"* the abuse.

Nonetheless, you might notice changes in a child's "usual" pattern of behaviour, such as being unusually irritated or avoidant of others when they had previously been reasonably regulated. Or they might display behaviour that the adults around them perceive to be challenging.

There may be physical, behavioural or psychological indicators that you could pick up on. The stronger your relationship with the child, the easier it may be to find the moments and spaces for connection where these indicators can be seen. However, even if you work very casually with the child, these indicators can still be seen and concerns shared.

Signs of psychological impact

Children who experience domestic abuse could show signs of:
- aggression and challenging behaviour
- depression
- anxiety
- changes in mood
- difficulty interacting with others
- fearfulness, including fear of conflict, fear of getting things wrong -
- suicidal thoughts or feelings
- self harm

All of which were previously explained in more detail, with regards to the possible ways in which they may present in a child, in Chapter Three.

There is also the possibility that this might all feel quite 'normal' to them depending on how long they have lived with domestic abuse.

"Towards the end you just get so numb...You're just, it's like you *accept it. I learnt to accept it, if this is going to be my life then there's no point in me complaining about it if I can't do anything about it. So, I might as well just carry on."* – 14 year old girl

Periods of transition or tribulation

We all, as families, experience highs and lows, with some degree of conflict or challenge. Many parents or carers experience challenging circumstances and continue to provide safety, love and care for their children. But as problems mount and pressures increase, it can be hard to maintain.

Periods of change, such as relocation, bereavement, pregnancy, nursing, job loss, separation etc bring about times where the whole family needs to transition, which increases the levels of conflict.

If a parent is already struggling with substance misuse or mental health problems, then managing conflict in a safe and healthy manner will already be hard enough. Therefore, in some cases, these additional factors contribute to or heighten the risk of significant harm from domestic abuse.

Whilst domestic abuse can take place in all kinds of homes, poverty is also a significant risk factor. Firstly and maybe more obviously, it adds to the pressure within a relationship. Secondly, women are disadvantaged within our economy, therefore more likely to be financially dependent and this is a very common reason why many women become trapped with an abuser. In fact, 97% of victims reported experiencing financially coercive control, according to Child Poverty Action Group UK.

ACTIVITY FOUR

Take some time to think about the children or families that you work with. How many of them are potentially at higher risk due to the aforementioned risk factors?

How many children are exposed to or have parents or carers who experience substance misuse? What is currently in place to support the family and safeguard the child from the impact of this?

How many children are exposed to or have parents or carers who experience mental health problems? What is currently in place to support the family and safeguard the child from the impact of this?

What measures are in place to support and listen to children during times of transition, such as relocation, bereavement, pregnancy, a new baby, job loss, separation?

Which national or local resources can we direct families to in times of hardship? How is your setting aware of which families are considered to be impacted by poverty?

Chapter Four Notes

Chapter Four Notes

Abuse grows from attitudes and values, not feelings. The roots are ownership, the trunk is entitlement, and the branches are control.
- Lundy Bancroft

CHAPTER FIVE

Responding to domestic abuse

Even if a victim of domestic abuse does not want to press charges against their abuser, the police may still decide to arrest them. Contrary to popular misconception, the victim's consent to press charges is not required when a police officer decides whether to arrest a suspect. Instead, the officer must have regard to the legal test for arrest set out in Section 24 of the Police and Criminal Evidence Act 1984. This means that in order to arrest a suspect the police officer must have knowledge or reasonable grounds for suspicion that

- an offence has taken place, is taking place, or is about to take place; and

- that the arrest is necessary

This understanding is relevant when considering child protection from the impact of domestic abuse because there is often a shared cynicism in many cultures, be those societal, workplace or otherwise. When people see a person being abused and repeatedly refuse (or, more appropriately, feel unable) to give evidence or access police intervention in the first place, those people can often misunderstand this barrier and/or become complacent to the abuse because their efforts may be futile. It is crucial for us to know that our efforts are never futile. We have the power to change the lives of victims and the children impacted by domestic abuse and we must use that power, regardless of the previous outcome. Firstly, because we never know when lasting change may occur, so not to give up hope. Secondly, because complacency sends a message to the victims and their children that they are worthy of the abuse and that no one is willing to support them. Fuelling their entrapment and further isolating them from relief.

Initial response

If the initial concern is in response to a direct disclosure from a child, the usual procedure for disclosures should be deployed. The key things that we do or do not do in response to a child disclosing abuse aim to:

- prevent the child from shutting down
  - remain calm
  - listen to what is being said without expressing shock or disbelief
  - avoid a display of denial to a child,
  - do not show shock or disgust at what they are saying
- prevent further trauma:
  - accept what the child says without judgement.
  - take it seriously
  - reassure the child
  - don't make promises that you can't be sure to keep, e.g. "we will make everything better now" and
  - don't promise confidentiality – never agree to keep secrets
  - tell the child that you will need to share this with people whose job it is to protect children
  - reassure the child that they did nothing wrong
  - ask the child how it felt coming to talk to you #

- obtain necessary information:
  - listen quietly, carefully and patiently
  - let the child explain to you in his or her own words what happened
  - do not make assumptions
  - do not investigate or interrogate
  - don't do anything that may jeopardise a police investigation
  - don't ask leading questions
  - do ask open questions like "tell me more about that"
  - communicate appropriately for their age, understanding and preference
  - do not ask the child to repeat what they have told you to someone else - you will do this
  - explain what you have to do next and specifically whom you have to talk to (according to your organisation's safeguarding policy)
  - do not discuss the case with anyone other than those named above

- share your concerns
  - make very brief notes at the time
  - write notes up in detail as soon as possible, using your organisation's safeguarding record keeping system
  - do not destroy your original notes in case they are required as evidence
  - record the date, time, place, the voice of (words used by) the child, including any swear words or slang
  - record how the child presented – be specific
  - record the facts, rather than your interpretations or assumptions

Reporting

> If you think a child is in immediate danger
> contact the police on **999**

If you are worried about a child but they are not in immediate danger, you have a duty to share your concerns.

- **Firstly, follow your organisational child protection procedure**. All organisations that work directly or indirectly with children and families must have safeguarding policies and procedures in place. You will need to use your setting's safeguarding record keeping system to pass on your concern safely and securely. Most organisations ask that you do this via a system but also report face to face with the safeguarding team if you have concerns that a child is at risk of or has suffered significant harm.
- **Contact your local safeguarding and child protection services**. All duty service contact details can be found on the website for the local authority that the child of concern lives in (this may be different to the authority that you work in).
- **If you are a safeguarding designated officer or deputy, you may require further support or guidance. Contact the NSPCC helpline** on 0808 800 5000 or by emailing help@nspcc.org.uk. Our trained professionals will talk through your concerns with you and give you expert advice.

The police and NSPCC helpline will both risk assess the situation and take appropriate action to protect the child. This may also include making a referral to the local authority.

ACTIVITY FIVE

SAFEGUARDING CHILDREN FROM DOMESTIC ABUSE

This activity is simply about information gathering, and checking in with who and where you may need to contact if you have concerns about a child experiencing domestic abuse.

Your organisational Safeguarding Officer is:

Name...................................Phone Number...........................
Your organisational Safeguarding Deputy is:

Name...................................Phone Number...........................

Your local safeguarding and child protection service is called:

..............................Phone Number...........................

Their "Out Of Hours" Service is available on................................

Your local domestic violence charity or service is called:

..............................Phone Number...........................

Your local domestic violence refuge is called:

..............................Phone Number...........................

Any other local services or contacts that come up in a search or from your Local Safeguarding Children's Board/Partnership Website:

Chapter Five Notes

Chapter Five Notes

As a victim of domestic violence, you live in a constant state of alertness and anticipation, waiting for the next attack to occur.

- Erin Sluka

CHAPTER SIX

Preventing domestic abuse

As professionals, and as citizens of the world, we all need to be committed to preventing domestic violence, by improving the support and protection for victims and their children and by bringing abusers to justice.

Awareness and Education

Women's Aid has committed to educating 2 million people by 2030 through their Abuse is Not Love campaign, by working in partnership with Yves Saint Laurent Beauty to educate children and young people about intimate partner violence.

The ☐Expect Respect Healthy Relationship Toolkit ☐produced by Women's Aid is a ☐brilliant prevention toolkit that enables professionals to hold conversations around the root causes that lead to violence. It is free to download and can be used by professionals in collaboration with children and young people.

Educating children about a multitude of mental wellbeing and personal development topics, from an early age, such as healthy relationships and conflict resolution, not only helps them to develop their emotional literacy but also provides an opportunity for them to reflect on the examples that they have been or currently see modelled at home. A safe and trusting environment would also allow the space for children to discuss and question their worldview.

Furthermore, when we are working with children and young people we subconsciously, or consciously if we choose, contribute to their understanding of power dynamics. Every challenge and task that we face with them holds the opportunity to demonstrate a power struggle or a collaboration. When our behaviour management approaches involve threats, even when disguised as rewards, coercion and a need for compliance we reinforce the idea that resolution is achieved through power and control. When we work restoratively with children through connection, play, curiosity, empathy and acceptance, we reinforce the idea that resolution is a collaboration and power can be shared.

Early help and early intervention

By supporting families in the right way at the right time (when challenges are initially identified) we, as practitioners can help to reduce the factors that contribute to or amplify domestic abuse. This requires services to take a multi-agency approach to early interventions for tackling root causes, such as mental health support, substance misuse support, housing and financial aid.

Early interventions that adopt an advocacy based approach have a more sustainable impact on victims, therefore signposting and increasing access to local domestic abuse charities or organisations is vital.

Another key element to getting *"the right support at the right time"* is a service's ability to be flexible in its delivery model, responding to the needs of families. Evidently, this is essential for supporting the engagement of, and fostering a sense of control for, families accessing help.

In all stages of intervention but crucially during early key worker-family relationship building, it is imperative to demonstrate high levels of confidentiality, reliability, respect and trust. Families, especially children, who have been impacted by domestic abuse are highly sensitive, hyper vigilant and can easily see through insincerity. Taking a therapeutic, trauma-informed, approach fosters trust and empowers them to facilitate positive change.

Positive family relationships

It's helpful, in some situations, for adults to learn more healthy ways to regulate their emotions and communicate with each other. This includes:

- reflecting on previous conflict and discussing what they could do differently next time
- developing healthier coping mechanisms and problem-solving strategies to help manage stress
- building skills for restorative communication and conflict resolution
- learning how to co-parent collaboratively

(Schrader McMillan and Barlow, 2019).

Restorative approaches to family culture are a great place to start. There are ways in which we can foster a restorative approach to everyday life, to conflict or challenge and to repair when harm has taken place. This is always based around the needs and emotions of the individuals involved.

Perpetrator Programmes

There are many National and local programmes available to support perpetrators through the process of changing their understanding, attitude and behaviour in regard to relationships. One project in particular campaigned since 2021, using the phrase "We need to stop asking "Why doesn't she leave?" and start asking "Why doesn't he stop?".

In April 2021, following a movement of over 125 expert organisations and individuals, the government set a legal requirement to publish a strategy for perpetrator programmes within a year.

Attention has since moved to the contents of the strategy and how it will complement comprehensive services for victims and survivors. Investments are required for *both* victim and perpetrator support and intervention – it should never be either/or. We also need interventions that accommodate all levels of risk.

Dr Brene Brown, a social work research scientist, famously says that *"when we are in pain and fear, anger and hate are our go-to emotions."* She encourages us to be mindful of our own internal narratives, *"When we lead, teach, or preach from a gospel of Viking or victim, win or lose, we crush faith, innovation, creativity, and adaptability to change."* This is crucial in our capacity to support families and even to lead within our organisations and our own families. Brown's research indicates that the *"key is to be vulnerable as people with other people. If we can't, we're either a Viking or a victim. Neither are good."*

Giving children a voice

People who work with children have a key role to play in identifying the signs of domestic abuse and reporting their concerns. Furthermore, they have a significant role in encouraging children to talk about their worries and concerns. Again I think it is essential to stress that the culture within our organisations has an essential role to play in making children feel safe enough to talk, to feel listened to, on a daily basis, and to feel that they are valued. I heard a great teacher once say that "If a child doesn't feel like they can bother the adults in your setting with the small stuff, they won't want to bother them with the big stuff either!".

Primary schools

Children need to be taught that abuse is never okay, and regularly reminded who they can talk to if they have any concerns, big or small. Schools have the opportunity to talk to children about all types of abuse, in an age-appropriate way.

I highly recommend the NSPCC "*Speak out, Stay safe*" service for primary schools, as it can be helpful in allowing children to understand what abuse is and know how to ask for help.

Secondary schools

In secondary schools, staff have the opportunity to talk in greater depth to children and young people about healthy relationships, and what they look, sound and feel like. Schools have a duty of care in terms of mental health and wellbeing, therefore should be cultivating an environment where young people feel safe and comfortable about reaching out for support.

Sports Clubs

In 2021 the government recognised the significance of out of school clubs including sports organisations, in terms of safeguarding and protecting children both within their own settings and in the wider context. Many sports clubs and other out of school services have improved their safeguarding standards and have made intentional efforts to help raise public awareness of safeguarding issues. A great example of this is a campaign called Football United Against Domestic Violence created by Women's Aid UK, who are working with national football bodies, sports media, football clubs, the police, players and fans to share a clear message that domestic violence is always unacceptable. Their aim is to call out any sexist behaviour which is a contributing factor to violence towards women and girls.

ACTIVITY SIX

What can you and/or your organisation do to reduce the risk of domestic abuse? Consider the following ideas and reflect on your own (organisational) practice:

How do you create a safe space to support the voices of children? What does this look like in terms of the "small things" and the "BIG"?

How do you raise awareness around safe conflict resolution? How does this reach those who may need it most? Children and adults?

How do you support a balanced narrative that includes both perspectives; abusers can modify their behaviour and victims of abuse can access the help and support they need to leave.

What does your perspective of the victim/Viking paradigm look like? How does this play out in your interactions with children and adults?

You already made a list of local support and early intervention services for domestic abuse. Consider how you may be able to build proactive working relationships with these services. Is there a way to build bridges from your community to these services so that reaching out in a time of crisis is easier? Make contact with some of these services and take note of your intentions.

Chapter Six Notes

Chapter Six Notes

The world suffers a lot. Not only because of the violence of bad people, but because of the silence of good people.
- Unknown

CHAPTER SEVEN

Supporting children who have been exposed to domestic abuse

It goes without saying that victims and survivors of domestic abuse need support, ongoing support. But for the purpose of this guide, we will focus, mostly, on children.

Nevertheless, it is essential to point out that for many victims of abuse, a shared concern is the fact that the majority of support is prescribed by someone in an office, limited to one or two interactions and extremely rigid in terms of time and space. This approach is not restorative and undermines the parent's capacity to safeguard her children and hinders their capacity to move beyond the abuse.

Over 60 % of referrals to victim refuge are refused. Furthermore, 45% of referrals to community based services are also refused. It is clear that nationally, we are unable to meet the demand in terms of domestic abuse victim support. But many success stories come from those victims who received restorative, flexible support from individuals who were involved. Supporting victims of domestic abuse (who are parents) in the right way, at the right time, increases both their capacity to create a safe, thriving environment for their children and improves our professional relationship with them to enable continued safeguarding.

So what can we do to support children directly? There are specialist support and services available for children and young people who are experiencing or have experienced domestic abuse.

Levels of Intervention

When we consider safeguarding and child protection, we use the terms *"Child in Need"* (referring to Section 17 of the Children's Act 1989) and *"Child Protection"* (referring to Section 17 of the Children's Act 1989) in reference to the level of need or intervention required to make a child's life safe and secure, in all regards.

Domestic violence is now considered an indicator that a child may be likely to suffer significant harm and therefore is in need. Different services will be required depending on the level of need of the child or children involved. The table below illustrates the suggestions for intervention, made by The Local Government Association (England).

Within this simplified model tier 1 considers all children - no additional needs, tier 2 considers vulnerable children - needing additional help, tier 3 considers children in need of intensive help, and tier 4 considers children at serious risk of harm who need complex help. This model has been adapted from the Hardiker, Exton and Barker model, LGConnect (2005).

Services for children and young people affected by domestic violence

Tier 4: **Acute/restorative** Children at risk of death or serious harm from an abusive parent or other	• Child protection services. • Police, court protection. • Alternative housing for abused parent and children. • Presumption of no contact. • Multi-agency risk management.
Tier 3: Complex Children whose lives are significantly disrupted by domestic violence	• Refuge, community based support. Accommodation options. • Advocacy and childcare services. • Supervised contact services. • Special education support. • CAMHS. • Counselling. • CIN Services – social services. • Multi-agency risk assessment.
Tier 2: Vulnerable **Children** Vulnerable due to domestic violence	• Access to community outreach. • Advocacy, group work and support services. Positive support from teachers, youth workers. • Information about domestic violence services. • Extended school provision. • Supported contact services. • Health visiting. • Therapeutic or restorative parenting. • Identification and referral within universal services.
Tier 1: All children Universal services.	• Antenatal assessment/routine questioning. • Health, Education etc. • PHSE. • Information about domestic violence. • Healthy relationship education.

When we, as practitioners and organisations, ensure good quality understanding and assessment of the risk around domestic violence, followed up with a tailored approach to the above services, we can make a significant difference to the lives of children and families. Children who experience domestic violence do not all need the same intervention and in fact, one child may need different levels of intervention at different times in their life, depending on the events that take place at home. This is to say that no child fits neatly into the model for the level of need and no child's needs remain the same, the reality is complex and ever changing.

The majority of Local Authorities have published their own guidance around the levels of need of children. This will give a further breakdown of what the levels of need look like, giving examples and references to specific risks or indicators of need. These do not negate professional judgement but do offer a means of clarity when sharing professional discussions. It is imperative that we, as practitioners, are familiar with the most up to date model that is employed by the authority/ies in which the children whom we work with reside. The Department of Health also offers national frameworks to support this.

To complement this Barnardo's Domestic Violence Outreach Service (DVOS) has developed a Domestic Violence Risk Assessment Model, which adds a system of threshold scales, risk factors, potential vulnerabilities and protective factors to the assessment process, enabling comprehensive analyses of risk. It aims to support practitioners in making decisions about the risks for children and planning appropriate interventions *with* the family. This model is underpinned by the following principles:

- Protecting children as first priority.

• Protecting non-abusing parent helps protect children.
• Providing supportive resources to parents helps protect children.
• Holding perpetrators responsible for abusive behaviour.
• Respecting non-abusing parents' right to autonomy without placing children at increased risk of abuse from domestic violence.

There are nine assessment areas in the DVOS risk assessment model, to assist professionals in reaching decisions about a child's vulnerability or need for protection.

The nine assessment areas are:
• Nature of abuse.
• Risks to the children posed by the perpetrator.
• Risks of lethality.
• Perpetrator's pattern of assault and coercive behaviours.
• Impact of the abuse on the women.
• Impact of the abuse on the children.
• Impact of the abuse on parenting roles.
• Protective factors.
• The outcome of the woman's past help-seeking.

This model, during studies, helped social workers to be clear and specific about the risks posed and decisions more informed. Research suggests that, when domestic violence is identified, the abused parent should be spoken to alone to understand and assess the specific risks that the perpetrator poses, and identify any protective steps which have been used in the past.

Professional Curiosity

The literature suggests that an abuser's tactics of domestic abuse and violence pose an additional threat to professionals.

Practitioners, working directly with the family, may be influenced by the same disempowerment that parental victims and children are exposed to. Careful supervision, safety protocols and the deployment of professional curiosity are key factors in ensuring that professionals are supported against threat or coercion. Professional curiosity encompasses an approach of respectfully exploring every possible indicator of abuse and an understanding of what day to day life for the child is like.

Action for Children

Action for Children is part of a group with expertise in children's issues, including domestic abuse and Violence Against Women and Girls. They have been working together to urge the Government to address the needs of children impacted by domestic abuse.

The Domestic Abuse Bill currently (2023) passing through UK Parliament is a crucial step in ensuring that children get the right help at the right time, in terms of protection from domestic abuse. The Bill is being called for to ensure that:

- Specialist support services for children are made available in all local areas.
- Frontline practitioners and public authorities recognise children as victims of the domestic abuse that occurs in their household.
- This could be achieved by changing the proposed statutory definition of domestic abuse to recognise that children experience domestic abuse too.

The NSPCC Domestic abuse, recovering together

Although the impact of experiencing domestic abuse can last into adulthood, many children are able to move forward when they are in a safer, more stable environment and have appropriate therapeutic support.

The DART programme, from the NSPCC, gives victims of domestic abuse and their children an opportunity to talk, learn to communicate effectively and to rebuild relationships. They also have the opportunity to meet other victims and children who have similar lived experiences and reflect together.

Operation Encompass

Operation Encompass is a safeguarding partnership, in England and Wales (Operation Encompass, 2021), between schools and the police that supports children who are exposed to domestic abuse.

Under the programme, police will inform a nominated child protection lead at a child's school if the child has been exposed to an incident of domestic abuse. This will take place before the start of the next school day to enable the school to put measures in place to support the child.

All child protection leads should attend a briefing to become aware of how the partnership works and develop their understanding of the impact of domestic abuse on children.

ACTIVITY SEVEN

What is your local guidance to the levels of need in terms of safeguarding and child protection called? Where is it available?

Who is your organisational designated safeguarding lead? Talk to them about Operation Encompass, can you get access to any briefings? What do you want to know about the partnership?

Who are your local child advocacy organisations? Write down their contact details below. If you couldn't access them, who could you work with within the community?

Chapter Seven Notes

Chapter Seven Notes

POSTFACE

Complacency may be the enemy of progress, but it's also the affirmation of poor choices.

I hate to hear people talk about hindsight when referring to child protection and in particular, domestic abuse.

"I knew something was off"
"I wish I had stepped in"
"I always thought they seemed scared to go home"

These are phrases that I have heard after the deaths of victims of domestic abuse. When the whispers become loud voices. People validate their concerns when the police tape lies visible for the village to see. But rarely when the cries and black eyes make the room feel uncomfortable.

We all have the power to improve the lives of the children and families around us. We have the opportunity to show victims *and* their children that they deserve more, that they can hold boundaries and that they are not alone in making the changes that are required to find safety.

POST GUIDE REFLECTIONS

How has this guidance changed your understanding of domestic abuse?

What changes do you wish to see, organisationally, to help reduce the risk to children from domestic abuse?

How will your practice be affected as a result?

How will your new practice make a difference to the lives of children and young people?

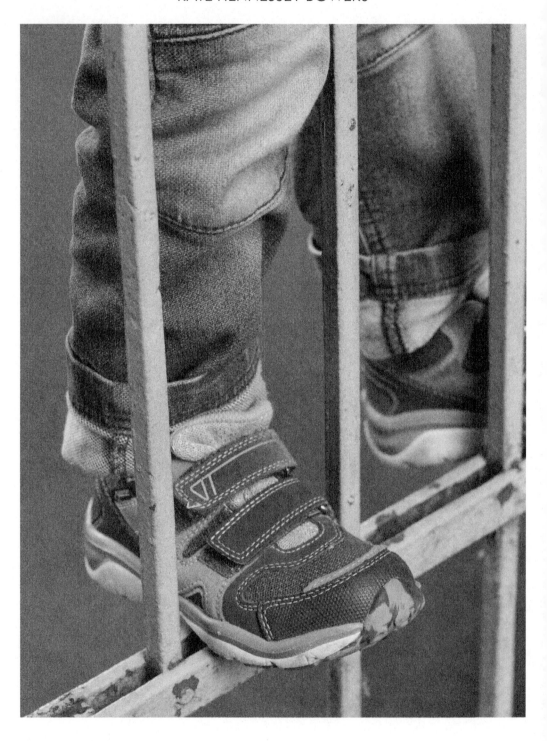

References and resources

Barter, C. (2009) In the name of love: partner abuse and violence in teenage relationships. British Journal of Social Work, 39(2): 211-233.

Brimicombe, A. and Cafe, R. (2012) Beware, win or lose: domestic violence and the World Cup. Significance, 9(5): 32-35.

Children's Commissioner, (2018) Voices of children living in households with domestic abuse, parental substance misuse and mental health issues. [Accessed 20/01/2023]

Child Poverty Action Group UK. Domestic Abuse Is An Economic Issue – For Its Victims And For Society. [Accessed 22/01/2023]

Coordinated Action Against Domestic Abuse, (2014) In plain sight, the evidence from children exposed to domestic abuse. (PDF) Bristol.

Department of Health, Social Services and Public Safety (DHSSPS) (2016) Stopping domestic and sexual violence and abuse in Northern Ireland: a seven year strategy (PDF). Belfast: DHSSPS.

Department of Health, Social Services and Public Safety (DHSSPS) and Department of Justice (2021) Stopping domestic and sexual violence and abuse in Northern Ireland strategy. [Accessed 20/01/2023].

Diez, C. et al (2018) Adolescents at serious psychosocial risk: what is the role of additional exposure to violence in the home? Journal of Interpersonal Violence, 33(6): 865-888.

Early Intervention Foundation, (Unknown).   [Accessed 20/01/2023]

Holt, S., Buckley, H. and Whelan, S. (2008). The impact of exposure to domestic violence on children and young people: a review of the literature. Child Abuse and Neglect, 32(8): 797-810.

Home Office (2022) Policy paper: tackling violence against women and girls strategy - update. [Accessed 21/01/2023].

Home Office (2021b) Domestic Abuse Bill 2020: factsheets. [Accessed 20/01/2023].

Home Office (2013) Definition of domestic violence and abuse: guide for local areas. [Accessed 20/01/2023].

Ivandic, R.; Kirchmaier, T. and Torres Blas, N. (2022) Football, alcohol and domestic abuse (PDF). CentrePiece (Spring 2022), 3-6.

Kirby, S., Francis, B. and O'Flaherty, R.(2013) Can the FIFA World Cup football (soccer) tournament be associated with an increase in domestic abuse? Journal of research in crime and delinquency, 51(3): 259–276.

LGConnect (2005). Vision for services for children and young people affected by domestic violence: Guidance to local commissioners of children's services.

NSPCC (2022) Children face greater risk of domestic abuse during World Cup. [Accessed 20/01/2023].

Office of National Statistics (2022) Data Collection and Statistical Returns, London. [Accessed 28/01/2023].

Operation Encompass (2021) Operation Encompass. [Accessed 20/01/2023].

Police Scotland and the Crown Office & Procurator Fiscal Service (2019) Joint protocol between Police Scotland and the Crown Office & Procurator Fiscal Service In partnership challenging domestic abuse (PDF). [Edinburgh]: Crown Office & Procurator Fiscal Service.

Schrader McMillan, A. and Barlow, J. (2019) Steps to safety: report on the feasibility study. London: NSPCC.

Scottish Government and Convention of Scottish Local Authorities (COSLA) (2018) Equally Safe: Scotland's strategy to eradicate violence against women. [Accessed 20/01/2023].

Shonkoff, J.P. et al (2008) The timing and quality of early experiences combine to shape brain architecture working paper 5. Cambridge: Center on the Developing Child, Harvard University.

Shonkoff, J.P. et al (2014) Excessive stress disrupts the architecture of the developing brain working paper 3. Cambridge: Center on the Developing Child, Harvard University.

Smith, E. (2016) Domestic abuse, recovering together (DART): evaluation report. London: NSPCC.

Sneddon, H and Janes, M (2017) Domestic Violence Risk Assessment for Children: Guidance Manual, Barnardo's Northern Ireland.

Stanley, N. (2011) Children experiencing domestic violence: a research review. Totnes: Research in Practice.

Szilassy, E. et al (2017) Making the links between domestic violence and child safeguarding: an evidence-based pilot training for general practice. Health and Social Care in the Community, 25(6): 1722-1732.

Welsh Government (2019) Domestic abuse, sexual violence and slavery: guidance for professionals. [Accessed 20/01/2023].

Women's Aid UK (2022) Expect Respect Healthy Relationships Toolkit [Accessed 24/01/2023]

Women's Aid UK (2022)The Impact of Domestic Abuse on Children and Young People [Accessed 20/01/2023]

HELPFUL RESOURCES

Refuge

Supports women and children who are experiencing, or have experienced, domestic violence or abuse.

You can call their helpline for support, information and advice - including help to access their emergency accommodation.

Online chat service available 3pm - 10pm, Monday - Friday.

You can send a message to the helpline using this online contact form (response time within 48 hours, or at a safe time chosen by you).

Opening times:

24 hours a day, every day of the year

0808 2000 247

NSPCC

Find out more about Speak Out Stay Safe

Information and advice for any adult concerned about the safety of a child.

Online contact form here.

Opening times:

8am - 10pm, Monday - Friday; 9am - 6pm at weekends

0808 800 5000

help@nspcc.org.uk

Childline

If a child or young person needs confidential help and advice direct them to Childline. Calls to 0800 1111 are free and children can also contact Childline online or read about domestic abuse on the Childline website. You can also download or order Childline posters and wallet cards.

Elearning

Our online and face to face courses can help to develop your understanding of when and how to protect children from domestic abuse and other forms of abuse.

You can find courses and more on our site by using the link:

https://syan.kartra.com/page/Links

You can find helpful books and resources on Amazon such as our Safeguarding Journal for note taking by following the link:

https://amzn.to/3YdTSq1

Where you can, also, click on the Kate Hennessey Bowers link to see other books written or created by Kate.

You can also find Kate on LinkedIn and Facebook if you would like to follow and connect.

Printed in Great Britain
by Amazon